/ klaʊdz /

Mary Buchinger

LILY POETRY REVIEW BOOKS

For Liam and Kai who showed me clouds

Michael: *When I was a hippie, I thought the sky was a mind.*

Mary: *It is.*

Contents

derivation / ˌder·ə'veɪ·ʃən /:

a daily ration; *whence cometh*;
watershed; meadow & muck;
begotten not made; testament
of continuance; pocked &
riven with scars & fissures;
purposeful foreplay; font of
significance; prone to flood;
whither thou goest; runnels of
sweat on the delta of a brow;
e n d l e s s movement;
movement away; pleated skirt;
whereas; Genesis; & etc.

/ ˈmɛər i /as in "a *Mary* of clouds"

begins with

the first syllable uttered by infants
opens into *ohm* through their lifetime;

invites; gives suckle;
sustains;

primary; holy; discovery
of body in the world;

love, both need & imperative;
understood; essential;

pirate;   ruthless;
overall   & first;

pronounced with a shake of the head;

nihilistic; won't go away;
what lasts & what itches;
irritant; infernal;

inescapable;
forked; probing; persistent;

opening of pathways; possibility;

how way leads on to way

/ ˈpɒk ɪt /as in "a *pocket* of clouds"

astrological fingerbowl; lipped &
jawed; ready to receive; to be
slipped into & out of; jingly
amassing of coinage & flash; ritual
rainmaker; indispensable;
dispenser of change & well-being;
frayed refuge; holey catch-all;
carrier of color; resistant to
airing; keeper of errors, one-offs
& strays; alternate cellar;
emily-marvelous-dickinson-
stitchery; vital; abiding

/ ˈkæm ə ˌsoʊl / as in "a *camisole* of clouds"

                          simultaneously there
      & not;

                          conjures a voyeur or
                          seeing with awareness of seeing;

                                              an aperture which excludes
                                              what it doesn't allow;

                 partial;

                                 (the   *i* alone is

                                 always somewhat,

                                 is   never   whole;

                                 requires   another

                                 for   depth   of

                                 perception);

                          finally & interminably both contained &
      incomplete;

                                 is not meant
          to be   seen

/ ˈlɪg ə mənt / as in "a *ligament* of clouds"

persistent linkage; *kapha*
& *dosha*, tension both
fruitful & necessary;
wrung out; bound by
hard facts; secret;
bespoken; may be
replaced or resurrected;
a series of relations &
begats; bears its history;
recoils easily & often;
capable of being
penetrated; articulate;
cross-forming &
intersectional; fibrous;
a watery fullness;
salamanderly true

/ ʌnˈræv əl /as in "an *unravel* of clouds"

           possibility backwards;

                           an a l p h a b e t
unworded
& stacked;
          potentiality bristled;

                                  searching & suggestive;

     devolution; what makes other
     & else possible; often
              experienced   as loss;   the together

     & the complete
             turned (memory); a journey
                   of   forgetting;   may   be
     serendipitous;

     heightens awareness of form
     vs. material;

     wrought   & unwrought, once
& again

/ haɪv /as in "a *hive* of clouds"

enviable   industry;

purposeful imbalance;   what whizzes off to

discover; sweet gold humming; furious; interdependent;

armed; jarring; consists of sticky propolis & populace; center

decentered; what is royal; inherited;   the shelter & the sheltered;

edible jewel; internal storm system;   settled with smoke or cold;

sun-made & driven; co-op; whole rolled   prairies & yellow

orchards   snug in its keep;   abundance;   winged cupbearers;

sea-sick; inventive language of movement & distance; easily stunned;

great; horde of hoarders; spinners of solstice;   intimate with blossom

/ ˌtær ənˈtɛl ə / as in "a *tarantella* of clouds"

midnight & carmine;
click & grind;
Dionysius & pals
(no pall);
piped hysteria;
spidery; unpopped
herky-jerky-
stomp-stomp;

(also,
what is beautiful
small, of a place, & precious)

/ grə'malkən/ as in "a *grimalkin* of clouds"

playful & discontent;
willfully soft; insinuating;

needful & kneading impulse;
sacrosanct; silly; glamour within its grasp;

easily squashed;
what chases make-believe & dust;

a measure of goodness;
filled with what does not break;

marked by prowess; capable of slaying;
genuine; yogic;
will not last

/ ˌflædʒ əˈleɪ ʃən / as in "a *flagellation* of clouds"

flung; Fahrenheit;
cloistered; caught;
muddled immolation;
dry scarlet indraw;
de-berried vines;
ponderous drape;
wracked; varicose;
vandalized; clawed;
whetted; banished;
unasked, received;
bidding, bitten;

/ swɪft / as in "a *swift* of clouds"

swirl of wing & tail;
        felt in the pit of the stomach or about the crown of the head;
          sure movement; sweet aroma;

    moth-ish; passing fancy; what is not weary; euphoric
  undertow; slicing of the sky in two,
in three,
  in infinity;

     tantric; a feather-tangled wind;
  embedded sound;

cross-hatched quickness;
        ever
   disappearing; what precedes
      knowledge; a chary

           capture; the last
             until

/ breɪd /as in "a *braid* of clouds"

wisp & bray & bellicose other;

extremities captured &

bound (as if)

concentrated dynamo; capable

of (self)destruction/instruction/suction;

tripart tango torqued

antennae or feeler;

uncut time-keeper;

twirling object

woven nest of earthen

tints; tender tent;

twisted whit

/ ˈtɪn səl ɹi / as in "a *tinselry* of clouds"

girlfriend gloss; rhinestone finery;   spangled mirror of

(soul);   polished spit;   crow's-nest jewel;   sun tart; tawdry

tic-toc;   butterfly wing;   heart flutter; incomplete asana;

shaped like a doorknob; turns for the sake of turning;

river, rock-bombed & noon-blazed;

alpine snow;
wished for & reviled;
too often underestimated;
fool's gold; gold

/ ˈsɒl ɪs / as in "a *solace* of clouds"

tatted with a sleek bone shuttle; opens like pages;
spreads like a cape; succoring adornment; downy; sagacious; perfumed;
beginning of the end of the beginning; hand-in-hand; incandescent
translucence; heft and hue of a full-grown lilac cat;
lemony; free, freeing, friable

/ trănz /as in "a *trans* of clouds"

              shifting; complete, yet not at all;

       movement as in *train*, but trackless without the *i*;

       snaky motion;

          indirect;

sly;

        a parting of the grass & sky;

          unpredictable, promise-full;

           is & is & is;

         is *with* God & *is* God;

the quality of breath attended;

        paper in flame;

            shoulder season;

  seasonal labor;

          full of wind & bluster;

           what precedes the rain;

mare's tail or mackerel

/ ˈoʊ ʃən /as in "an *ocean* of clouds"

the end   of striving;
salt; orgasm;   culmination; what is godly;
mid-gut utterance   with a fullness of air & sound;
bears the quality of being   life-sustaining; changeable; unreliable;
able to pound & destroy seemingly   without malice; grasping; buoys up;
undermines; both full & empty; *what giveth   & what taketh away;* he & she & they;
the everyness of sexual being; encompasses   what is possible; *this too   this too   this too*

/ myul /as in "a *mewl* of clouds"

what calls; plaintive; bored;

whine

against the void;

stricken; suggestive;

test of an audience;

voiced yearning; flush with stripe & variation;

improvised; reedy batik;

crescendo & apex;

roams unharnessed;

belies a pragmatic

constitution;

moody; piecemeal summoning

of a world & its inhabitants;

what is not-contentment;

covert lightning; grating or tender;

ripened

apathy;

magnifies silence

/as in "an *absence* of clouds"

the nothing that suggests   something in the way
hunger manifests a gut;   shaped like a bowl
with neither sides nor bottom;   often echoes
like a howl, or rings like tinnitus;   end of
a concert; the gap between the pickets   of a
fence that renders a fence picket; the   four
a.m. street; the moment in which an *I* parts;
      already, in what has left shore, the new wave
begins; sometimes perfect

/ ˌmɜr mə ˈreɪ ʃən / as in "a *murmuration* of clouds"

unruly desire; ambivalent
    awakening; a whirring
into sight
  not to be
      ((doubted; ((impossible
  to prove; paisley'd dance
    of dependence—inter- &
nonce)
tempest
    of being|s;
gorge
  ous &
    pre
        carious
            con
          gre
        ga
            tion

/ ˈlæn tərn /as in "a *lantern* of clouds"

photonic
tocsin; cousin of
the celestial;   swings
revelatory; searching & circum-
spect; preceded by its a u r a;
severs sleep;   inherently quenchable;
convent of lumen & dazzle; sequestered;
tossable knockabout;

epi
phan
ous;

limned & limning;
easily lit easily shattered

/ ˌrɛz ə ˈrɛk ʃən / as in "a *resurrection* of clouds"

what is again & again & again & again & again;

buoyant repetition; boundless & fulfilling; intimate

with death; scathed; has known the end of green &

the earliest light; a blinding & absolute refusal;

essence of revocability; what has been given & taken

away & given again; a raising up as in a wall or a life;

a calling back; a return to something other than

home; a lift of the spirit; an undermining of the

status quo; roundly revolutionary; in form: a rhotic

anchor & rudder, scintillating sibilants—bone-in-the-

throat—diversion-through-open-passages; in content:

a trip to hell & back & back & back; this the only life

we'll know we know; what means both now &

for now; unwarranted cloak of grace, sometimes

suffocating; whiff of sulfur, washed anew

NOTES

In this collection, the notation that appears between slashes is a phonetic representation using the International Phonetic Alphabet (IPA), which "is an alphabetic system of phonetic notation based primarily on the Latin script. It was devised by the International Phonetic Association in the late 19th century as a standardized representation of speech sounds in written form. The IPA is used by lexicographers, foreign language students and teachers, linguists, speech–language pathologists, singers, actors, constructed language creators and translators" (from Wikipedia).

derivation / ˌder·ə'veɪ·ʃən / includes references to Psalms 121, verse 1: "I will lift up mine eyes unto the hills, from *whence cometh* my help" and Ruth 1, verse 16: "And Ruth said, Intreat me not to leave thee, or to return from following after thee: for *whither thou goest*, I will go; and where thou lodgest, I will lodge: thy people shall be my people, and thy God my God."

/ 'mɛər i / as in "a *Mary* of clouds": *how way leads on to way* is from Robert Frost's poem, "The Road Not Taken."

/ 'pɒk ɪt / as in "a *pocket* of clouds": Emily Dickinson sewed pockets on her dresses to carry a pencil and notebook.

/ 'lɪg ə mənt / as in "a *ligament* of clouds": *Kapha dosha* is the combination of earth and water according to the Ayurveda philosophy.

ACKNOWLEDGEMENTS

Grateful acknowledgment is due to the editors of the following publications in which these poems, some in earlier versions, first appeared:

Gargoyle: / swɪft / as in "a *swift* of clouds"

Laurel Review: / ˈkæm ə ˌsoʊl / as in "a *camisole* of clouds"

Lily Poetry Review: / haɪv / as in "a *hive* of clouds"

Pedestal: / ˌrɛz əˈrɛk ʃən / as in "a *resurrection* of clouds"

Permafrost: / myul / as in "a *mewl* of clouds"

Phoebe: / trănz / as in "a *trans* of clouds"

Seneca Review: / breɪd / as in "a *braid* of clouds"

South Dakota Review: / ˌm3r məˈreɪ ʃən / as in "a *murmuration* of clouds;"

   / ˈmɛər i / as in "a *Mary* of clouds;"

   / ˈoʊ ʃən / as in "an *ocean* of clouds"

Sugar House Review: / ˈtɪn səl ri / as in "a *tinselry* of clouds;"

   / ˈæb səns / as in "an *absence* of clouds"

First and foremost, thanks to my earliest teachers— Mrs. Barcalow, Daniel Thurber, Phil Legler, Marmo Soemarmo, Harold Bond— who inspired me to relish the expansive possibilities of language and words. Thanks to Danielle Legros Georges, Ravi Yelamanchili, Anne Riesenberg, Andrea Read, Heather Hughes, Bert Stern, Tam Neville, Mel Shorin, and Michael Mack, who read first drafts of these strange poems and encouraged me to keep going. Thanks too, to my workshop partners in the New England Poetry Club for their insights and to Michael Shapiro for helping me better understand this project. I'm thankful for my son Liam's eye and art— his photograph of his sculpture captures the suppleness of material and light. What a joy to have our work appear together! I'm grateful for the Mass Ave. bridge which allows me views of the clouds over the Charles River on my walk to school. The generous grant of a sabbatical helped make this work possible— my thanks to Provost Caroline Zeind, Dean Delia Anderson, and the Massachusetts College of Pharmacy and Health Sciences. Profound gratitude to Eileen Cleary for her fierce compassion and open-hearted faith in poetry. Finally, always and ever, these poems and I have benefitted from the care and attention of Hilary Sallick and Linda Haviland Conte. I am so grateful for their steadfast friendship and wisdom. Love and thanks in abundance to Steve, Liam, Kai, Dover, Couloir, and Dunya.

ABOUT THE AUTHOR

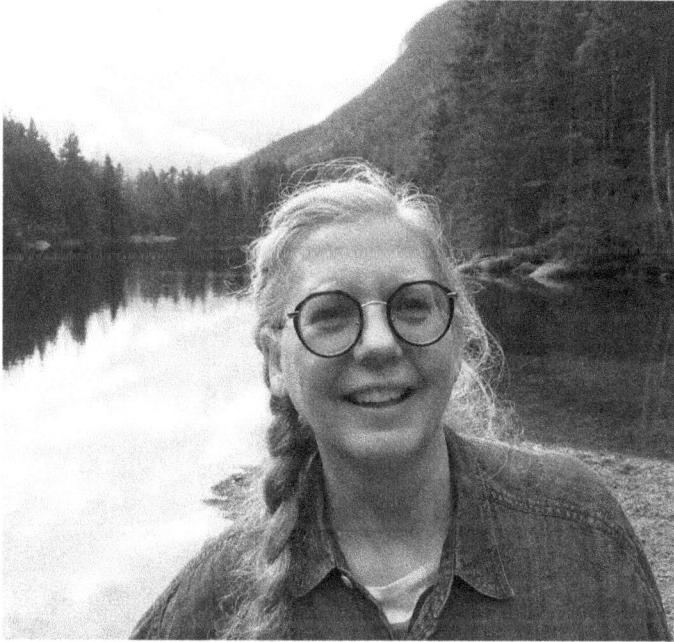

Author photo: Stephen Bodwell

Mary Buchinger is the author of *e i n f ü h l u n g/in feeling* (Main Street Rag, 2018), *Aerialist* (Gold Wake, 2015, finalist for the May Swenson Poetry Award, semifinalist for The Journal /Wheeler and Perugia Press Prizes), *Navigating the Reach* (forthcoming, Salmon Poetry), and *Virology* (forthcoming, Lily Poetry Review Books). She grew up in rural Michigan, volunteered in Ecuador for the Peace Corps, earned a doctorate in linguistics from Boston University. President of the New England Poetry Club and professor at the Massachusetts College of Pharmacy and Health Sciences, she lives in Cambridge with her husband, dog, and cats.

www.ingramcontent.com/pod-product-compliance
Lightning Source LLC
Chambersburg PA
CBHW080603030426
42336CB00019B/3308